Science & Technology

Jane Bingham

Raintree

www.raintreepublishers.co.uk
Visit our website to find out more information about **Raintree** books.

To order:
☎ Phone 44 (0) 1865 888113
🖹 Send a fax to 44 (0) 1865 314091
🖥 Visit the Raintree bookshop at **www.raintreepublishers.co.uk** to browse our catalogue and order online.

First published in Great Britain by Raintree,
Halley Court, Jordan Hill, Oxford OX2 8EJ,
part of Harcourt Education.

Raintree is a registered trademark of Harcourt Education Ltd.

Editorial: Isabel Thomas and Rosie Gordon
Design: Richard Parker & Tinstar Design www.tinstar.com
Picture Research: Hannah Taylor and Zoe Spilberg
Production: Duncan Gilbert

Originated by Chroma Graphics
Printed and bound in China by South China Printing Company

10-digit ISBN 1 406 20154 5
13-digit ISBN 978 1 4062 0154 3

10 09 08 07 06
10 9 8 7 6 5 4 3 2 1

British Library Cataloguing in Publication Data
Bingham, Jane
    Science and technology. - (Through artists' eyes)
    1.Science in art - Juvenile literature 2.Technology in art
    - Juvenile literature 3.Art - History - Juvenile literature
    I.Title
                704.9495

Acknowledgements
The publishers would like to thank the following for permission to reproduce photographs: **p. 40**, © 1995, Photo Scala, Florence/ Musee d'Orsay; **p. 13**, © 2004, Photo The Newark Museum/ Art Resource/ Scala, Florence; **p. 49**, © 2005, Digital Image, The Museum of Modern Art, New York/ Scala, Florence; **p. 41**, © ADAGP, Paris and DACS, London 2006 Photo: Bridgeman Art Library/ Private Collection, © Lefevre Fine Art Ltd., London; **p. 44**, © DACS 2006 Photo: Bridgeman Art Library/ Civica Galleria d'Arte Moderna, Milan, Italy; **p. 25**, © Salvador Dali, Gala-Salvador Dali Foundation, DACS, London 2006 Photo: 2005. Digital Image, The Museum of Modern Art, New York/ Scala, Florence; **p. 48**, © Salvador Dali, Gala-Salvador Dali Foundation, DACS, London 2006 Photo: Bridgeman Art Library/ Museum Boymans van Beuningen, Rotterdam, The Netherlands, © Christie's Images; **p. 23**, © The Andy Warhol Foundation for the Visual Arts, Inc./ ARS, NY and Dacs, London 2006 Photo: ©2000. Photo The Andy Warhol Foundation/ Art Resource/ Scale, Florence; **p. 45**, © The Estate of Roy Lichtenstein/ DACS 2006 Photo: Bridgeman Art Library/ Scottish National Gallery of Modern Art, Edinburgh, UK; **p. 47**, © The Estate of Roy Lichtenstein/ DACS 2006 Photo: Tate Picture Library; **p. 20**, akg-images; **p. 32**, akg-images / British Library; Bridgeman Art Library/ **pp. 19**, (© Ashmolean Museum, University of Oxford, UK), **43**, (© Leeds Museums and Galleries (City Art Gallery) U.K), **33** (Bibliotheque des Arts Decoratifs, Paris, France, Archives Charmet), **37**, (Broadlands Trust, Hampshire, UK), **p. 35**, (Jefferson College, Philadelphia, PA, USA), **4**, (Mauritshuis, The Hague, The Netherlands), **21**, (Mucha Trust), **28**, (National Gallery, London, UK), **18**, (Private Collection); **p. 8**, Corbis Royalty Free; **p. 46**, Kunstmuseum, Basel/ Martin Bühler; **p. 29**, Mary Evans Picture Library; **p. 12**, Photography © The Art Institute of Chicago; **p. 50**, Ronald Grant Archive/ ROY EXPORT COMPANY; **p. 5**, Science Picture Library/ David Scharf; **p. 26**, Sonia Halliday Photographs; **p. 39**, Tate Picture Library; **p. 14**, The Ancient Egypt Picture Library; **p. 15**, The Art Archive / Abbey of Novacella or Neustift / Dagli Orti; **p. 11**, The Art Archive / British Library; The Art Archive **pp. 17** (British Library), **42**, (Laurie Platt Winfrey), **27**, (National Museum Damascus Syria / Dagli Orti), **31**, (Private Collection / Dagli Orti); **p. 38**, The National Gallery, London; **p. 24**, Werner Forman Archive; **p. 6**, Werner Forman Archive/ Dr E. Strouhal; **p. 9**, Werner Forman Archive/ Museum fur Volkerkunde, Berlin.
Cover: *Stacks in Celebration*, 1954 (oil on canvas), Sheeler, Charles (1883-1965) reproduced courtesy of Bridgeman Art Library/ The Dayton Art Institute, Dayton, Ohio, USA, Museum Purchase.

The publishers would like to thank Karen Hosack for her assistance in the preparation of this book.

Contents

Any words that appear in bold, **like this**, are explained in the glossary.

Introduction

You have travelled back in time to 17th century Holland. You've stumbled into a dimly lit room, and suddenly you realize … you're watching a science lesson.

Seven solemn figures are grouped around a dead body, while a learned professor delivers his lecture. The teacher holds a pair of silver tongs and uses them to display the **tendons** in a dead man's arm. Some of the group look up, staring you straight in the eye, but the others continue to gaze at the **dissected** arm. There is an atmosphere of great concentration – this is clearly an important occasion.

In fact, what Rembrandt van Rijn was showing in this famous painting was Dr Nicholas Tulp delivering a lecture on human **anatomy**. When the young artist was invited to paint the surgeon Doctor Tulp, he decided not to produce a standard portrait. Instead, Rembrandt chose to show the great doctor at his work. Rembrandt had studied human anatomy while he was a student, and his painting reveals his fascination with the study of the human body.

Rembrandt's careful and accurate treatment of his subject also reflects the growing public interest in science in the early 17th century. His painting caused a sensation when it was first exhibited.

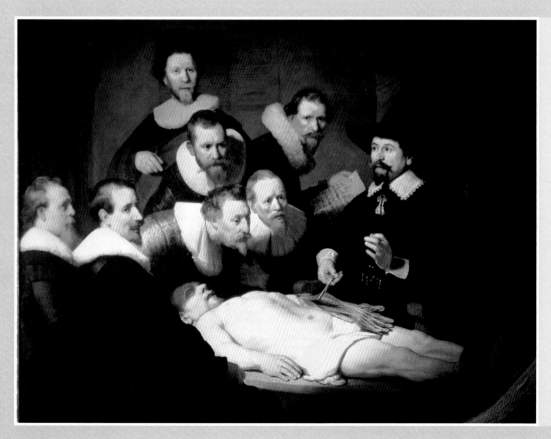

Rembrandt van Rijn, *The Anatomy Lesson of Dr Tulp* (1632). This famous painting has been seen as a public statement of Rembrandt's interest in science. The details of the dissected arm are remarkably accurate, revealing the artist's strong knowledge of human anatomy.

Looking at science and technology

This book looks at science and technology through artists' eyes. It traces the history of science and technology through time, starting with early inventions such as the wheel. Then it looks at discoveries in a number of different areas. These different fields of discovery range from building, printing, and time keeping, to transport and computer technology.

Throughout history, artists have responded to new discoveries in science and technology. Sometimes an artist shows a new invention – such as a train, or a telephone. Sometimes, artists picture people making discoveries. Often, an invention is simply shown in use, as artists produce images of builders using special tools, or people driving cars.

Using inventions

As well as showing new inventions, artists make use of new technology in their art. This book shows how artists have used new techniques in printing, photography, and computer technology. It also describes the ways that **architects** have used new construction techniques and inventions to create great works of art.

A range of art

This book starts with **prehistoric** cave paintings and ends in the 21st century. It ranges across the world, covering painting and sculpture, but also includes architecture, literature, and photography. To help you see exactly where a work of art was made there is a map of the world on page 52. There is also a timeline on page 53. This provides an overview of the different periods of history discussed in this book.

A highly magnified image of a fly, by David Scharf. Scharf is a scientist and artist who specializes in images viewed through an electronic microscope, then coloured.

Early discoveries

Over 100,000 years ago, our ancient ancestors made a very important discovery. They worked out how to make a hunting spear by fixing a sharpened flint to a wooden shaft. With the help of this basic tool, they could kill wild animals for food.

Hunters with spears are shown in **prehistoric** cave paintings dating from around 30,000 years ago. Some later cave paintings show how hunting technology gradually developed. By 20,000 BCE, painters were showing hunters using bows and arrows, knives, and spears.

This painting of farming life in Ancient Egypt shows the farmers using simple technology – a metal scythe for cutting the corn, and a wooden plough.

Pots and ploughs

After the invention of hunting weapons, the next major discovery was the craft of pottery. Around 13,000 years ago, people began moulding clay into pots. These pots could be used for storing food and water, and also for cooking food over a fire. Pots have been found in the Middle East, dating from around the 5th century BCE. They show a high level of skill, but they are not just useful objects. They are also works of art, decorated with striking **geometric** patterns.

Around the same time that people were discovering how to make pots, the plough was invented. Early ploughs were simple wooden tools pulled by oxen. The plough was a very important piece of equipment for the Ancient Egyptians, and it is often shown in Egyptian paintings of farming life. Some Ancient Egyptian artists also made models of oxen pulling ploughs. No one is sure what these models were for. They may have been placed in graves, or they may have been children's toys.

Using wheels

In very early societies, people dragged heavy loads in wooden sledges, or used a series of logs to roll stone blocks along the ground. Then, around 3500 BCE, some people in Ancient Sumeria (in present-day Iraq) came up with a new way to transport heavy weights. They fixed wheels onto their sledges to help them move along. Some very early wheels are shown in a **mosaic** panel known as the "Standard of Ur". The panel shows warriors riding in chariots with solid wooden wheels.

Inspiration from pots?

Some experts think that the wheel was invented by potters. Sumerian pots are very regular in form, and they were probably made using a potter's wheel. After the potter's wheel had been invented, it was only a matter of time before people began to fix wheels onto crates, to make carts.

Building and engineering

Building and construction began very simply. Early people built basic shelters to keep themselves warm and safe. These early shelters were usually made from wood. However, by the time of the Ancient Egyptians, people had made great progress in construction.

Egyptian pyramids

Around 2600 BCE, the Ancient Egyptians began to build vast stone pyramids in the desert. These amazing structures were so well built that many of them are still standing today. **Archaeologists** believe that the pyramids were built without the help of scaffolding, **pulleys**, or **winches**. They think that ramps were built up the side of the pyramids, to help builders lift the stones into place. Then, the pyramid was constructed layer by layer, getting smaller and smaller towards the top. Finally, a thin shell of stone was added to each side of the pyramid, giving it a smooth, triangular outline.

With their dramatic, triangular form, the Egyptian pyramids are stunning works of art. However, the unusual shape of the pyramids is really the result of the Egyptians' limited technology. Without the help of any machines for lifting stones, it was impossible to build tall buildings straight upwards, so they needed a slope.

The Ancient Egyptian pyramids are spectacular examples of early architecture. In order to make each triangular face match precisely, the Egyptians must have had a good understanding of geometry.

Roman buildings

The Roman civilization began in the 8th century BCE, and lasted for over a thousand years. The Romans constructed entirely different buildings from the Egyptians. With the help of winches and cranes, they built tall buildings with arches and sturdy columns.

The Romans copied the building skills from the Ancient Greeks, but added new inventions of their own. They discovered how to build rounded arches. They also invented an early form of concrete, a mixture of volcanic ash, water, and stones. These two discoveries meant that the Romans could construct massive, multi-storey buildings, such as the **Colosseum** in Rome.

A few carvings survive showing Roman builders at work, using a range of tools, cranes, and winches. One carving from the tomb of a wealthy builder features an enormous crane, which is worked by men walking inside it. The Roman **sculptors** show the details of tools and machinery with care. They are clearly fascinated by the technology of the builders' craft.

Pyramids in the Americas

The Egyptians were not the only people to build pyramids. Around 100 BCE, the people of Teotihuacán in present-day Mexico built vast pyramids dedicated to the Sun and Moon. Later, the Maya and the Aztec people continued the tradition of pyramid building in Central America. Mayan carvers decorated each level of their pyramids with carved and painted scenes.

An Aztec clay model of a temple, built in the form of a pyramid. Many early American people used the pyramid form in their architecture.

Medieval builders

During the **Middle Ages**, people in Europe constructed some astonishing buildings. They built massive castles with sturdy walls to stand up to enemy attacks. They also constructed beautiful cathedrals, with delicate stained-glass windows and soaring spires.

Building a castle or cathedral was an enormous job. It could take over a century to finish a cathedral, and sometimes hundreds of people worked together on a site. Fortunately, some artists made a visual record of these building projects. Their paintings show crowded scenes filled with activity.

Paintings of builders

Paintings of **medieval** building projects usually show a wide range of workers, each with their own specialist tools. Stonemasons use a **chisel** and **mallet** to cut large blocks of stone, while "roughmasons" lay the stones, applying **mortar** with a trowel. Meanwhile, carpenters saw up logs, and use hammers and wooden pegs to construct scaffolding, window frames, and doors.

Scurrying around are labourers carrying loads on carts and stretchers, while the "master mason" is usually shown in the centre of the scene, giving orders. In some paintings, the master mason holds a large wooden **set-square** in his hand. This was part of the equipment that he used to draw up his plans.

Many paintings of building scenes include the striking outline of a large wooden crane, perched on a high scaffolding platform. These simple machines had a large wooden wheel and were used to haul up buckets, attached to a rope. Building in the Middle Ages must have been very dangerous work, but the element of danger is not shown in the paintings. Instead, the artists concentrate on how all the workers co-operate together.

Medieval images of building work are not always very skilful, but the different activities are carefully observed. The artists manage to convey a sense of the drama and excitement of the massive building projects of the Middle Ages.

An architectural sketchbook

During the 13th century, a Frenchman called Villard de Honnecourt produced a remarkable sketchbook. The book includes detailed drawings of **architectural** features, such as arches and columns. It also contains ground plans for buildings, and sketches of machinery, such as a giant saw and a simple crane. Some people think that Villard was a master mason. Others think he was an artist. Either way, he was fascinated by architecture and construction.

This medieval **manuscript** painting shows builders at work. The tower has been covered with wooden scaffolding, and a large winch is used to raise heavy blocks of stone.

Building with steel

In the 19th century, engineers and architects began to work with steel. Steel is light-weight but very strong, and it allowed people to build much larger, more adventurous structures than before. Engineers built bridges for roads and railways, using steel **girders** and cables. Meanwhile, some imaginative architects designed buildings from steel.

Many artists responded with delight to the new structures, painting them from many angles. They found some exciting ways to show the bold, new buildings.

A tower and a bridge

The Eiffel Tower was a spectacular early steel building. It was completed in 1889 for an international exhibition in Paris. The French artist Robert Delaunay painted the Eiffel Tower many times. He was excited by the tower's new materials and dramatic shape, and also by the fact that it was a centre for radio **communications**. In *The Red Tower* (1912), Delaunay shows a scarlet Eiffel Tower against a collection of swirling blue and grey shapes. The soaring tower dominates the painting, and seems to be the source of all the city's energy.

Robert Delaunay, *The Red Tower* (1912). Delaunay produced several paintings of the Eiffel Tower, with its red-coloured paint. He saw the red tower as an exciting symbol of the modern world. The style that he used to show the tower reflects his sense of excitement.

Joseph Stella lived close to Brooklyn Bridge in New York. He produced many paintings of the bridge, which he saw as a symbol of a hopeful future. To Stella, the bridge was a "shrine containing all the efforts of the new civilization of America". In *Old Brooklyn Bridge* (1941), Stella shows the bridge at night. Cables soar overhead, traffic signals and headlights flash through the darkness, and the bridge's pointed arches rise in the background like the arches of a church.

City skyscrapers

By the start of the 20th century, architects were using a combination of concrete and steel to build towering skyscrapers. Many early skyscrapers were built in the city of New York. Structures like the Chrysler Building and the Empire State building can be regarded as works of art in their own right. With their soaring pinnacles, and gleaming walls and windows, they express a spirit of hope and excitement.

Many painters have attempted to capture the spirit of skyscrapers. Georgia O'Keeffe's *Radiator Building* (1927) shows one of New York's famous early skyscrapers at night. The partly-lit windows form an intriguing, geometric pattern, and spotlights pick out the details on the roof, giving the building a sense of magic, power, and mystery. Charles Sheeler's painting *Windows* (1952) shows the block-like shapes

of skyscrapers from below. Here, the soaring towers with their blank windows seem bleak and threatening, like towering cliffs.

Brooklyn Bridge study from Joseph Stella, *The Voice of the City of New York Interpreted* (1920–1922). This series of paintings celebrates the energy of New York City, with its soaring architecture.

Writing and printing

Writing was invented around 5,000 years ago in Ancient Sumeria. The Ancient Sumerians developed a form of picture writing, using symbols which each had a special meaning. This basic form of writing was adapted by the Ancient Egyptians, who created a range of symbols, known as **hieroglyphs**.

Egyptian artists carved and painted hieroglyphs on tomb and palace walls. **Scribes** kept records on wax tablets. The Egyptians also discovered how to make a kind of paper from reeds. This early paper is known as "papyrus". All these developments marked the start of the art of writing.

Egyptian scribes

Several carvings and statues showing scribes at work survive from Ancient Egyptian times. In most of these works, the scribe sits cross-legged with a wax tablet on his lap, and a simple pointed stick called a "stylus" in his hand.

One striking statue shows the scribe of the temple of Karnak gazing proudly ahead, with a papyrus **scroll** spread over his knees. His name is recorded on the base of the statue, showing that the scribe was a highly respected figure in Egyptian society.

Carved hieroglyphs from an Ancient Egyptian monument. One of the symbols carved here is a scribe's feather pen.

Roman writing

By the time of the Roman Empire, the art of writing was flourishing. Business records were written on papyrus. People carved inscriptions in stone, and poems and plays were written on pages of vellum, which was made from the skin of young goats, lambs or calves. Roman carvings show children learning to write at school, using a metal stylus and a wax tablet.

Educated Romans clearly took pride in their ability to write. One famous Roman portrait shows a young couple, both proudly displaying their own writing equipment. The man holds a scroll while his wife has a stylus and tablet.

Medieval manuscripts

In the Middle Ages, Christian monks created exquisite illuminated **manuscripts**. They copied out texts in beautiful script and illustrated them with paintings, known as "illuminations". The monks used **pigments** made from earths and minerals, including some brilliant blues, scarlets, and greens. They mixed the powders with egg whites and other substances to make them stick to the page. They also "gilded" their pages with very fine layers of gold and silver leaf.

Manuscript illuminations were often decorated letters, or images around text. However, artists soon began to paint complete scenes. This was the start of the art of painting in the West.

Detail from *Missal of Stephane Stettner and Abbot Auguste Posch* (1526). Monks copied out texts by hand and decorated their texts with delicate patterns and flowers. The first letter of a text was often "illuminated" by a miniature painted scene, as seen here.

Chinese paper

Around the year 100 CE, paper was invented in China. Sheets of paper were made by dipping a bamboo screen into a mixture of pulped tree bark, plants, and rags. Then a thin layer of paper pulp was left to dry on the screen. Unlike vellum and parchment, Chinese paper was both cheap to produce and easy to write on.

At first, the Chinese used paper to make panels that could be rolled up like a scroll or hung on walls. These long and narrow paper panels were used for writing out official documents, but they were also used by artists. Chinese artists developed a style of painting to fit on the scrolls. They showed flowers, birds, and landscapes with a small amount of text running down the side of the painting.

Woodblock printing

The Chinese not only invented paper. They were also the first people to discover the art of printing. Printing was used as early as the 6th century. In 593 CE, the Chinese emperor ordered the printing of **Buddhist** images and **scriptures**.

Chinese printers created woodblocks for each page. Text and images were written and drawn on a piece of thin paper, then glued face down onto a wooden block. Then the characters and images were

carved into the wood to make a printing plate. This was dipped in ink and used to print the text.

Making silk

As well as painting on paper, Chinese artists painted on panels made from silk. A painted silk scroll dating from the 13th century illustrates the process of making silk. It shows workers collecting **cocoons** spun by **silk worms**, laying the cocoons on trays, and unwinding their silky threads.

The Diamond Sutra

One of the world's earliest surviving printed works is the *Diamond Sutra*. It was printed in China in 868 CE and contains a Buddhist text illustrated by a large and detailed drawing.

The picture in the *Diamond Sutra* shows the figure of the Buddha surrounded by his followers and other spirits. The artist has used clear, flowing lines. No white gaps are left in the picture, and every part of the scene is filled with detail.

The Chinese discovered woodblock printing over 500 years before people in the West. The *Diamond Sutra*, shown here, was made in 868 BCE. By this time, craft workers in China had become expert at carving woodblocks for printers.

The printing press

In 1436, Johannes Gutenberg invented the printing press in Germany. Gutenberg's machine worked by pressing a sheet of paper onto a printing block that had been filled with letters and covered with ink. Using Gutenberg's press, people could print the same page hundreds of times. This meant they could produce books quickly and cheaply. The printing press had a huge impact on European society, as it meant that ideas could spread very rapidly.

Several images of early presses have survived. Early images of printing presses show a massive wooden structure, with a heavy wooden press, which had to be pushed down firmly by its operator.

Woodcuts and engravings

By the 1450s, printing presses had been set up all over Europe, and books of all sorts began to be produced. Many of these books were illustrated by simple line drawings, which were carved into wooden blocks covered with ink. Early woodblock prints, often known as "woodcuts", relied on bold designs for their effect. They were usually fairly crudely drawn, with very little shading.

St Jerome in his study pulling a thorn from a lion's paw, first illustration in a collection of *St Jerome's letters* (1492). In the picture are examples of the older technology of handwritten manuscripts.

About 20 years after the printing press was invented, artists discovered "engraving". They scratched designs into copper plates. The plates were covered with ink and printed onto sheets of paper. This made pictures. Engravers used a sharp, pointed tool to carve their lines into the copper. Depending on the amount of pressure they used, the line could be very fine, or wide and deep. This technique was difficult, but it could produce very delicate results.

Dürer's masterpieces

The German artist Albrecht Dürer made woodcuts and engravings in the late 15th century. Unlike many earlier woodcuts, Dürer's are incredibly detailed. His famous study of a rhinoceros shows every detail of the creature's skin. Dürer's engravings are even more detailed. In his scene of a knight riding through a wood, each texture is represented in its own way, so that the horse's coat, the knight's shining armour, and the leather of his boots all look entirely different.

Japanese woodcuts

In the 18th century, print-makers in Japan developed a technique for making coloured woodcuts. Japanese artists created bold and dramatic prints, with large areas of flat colour. These striking works of art influenced many artists in Europe and America.

Hiroshige, *Suigin Grove and Masaki, on the Sumida River* (1865). Hiroshige's bold designs and delicate use of colour inspired many painters and print makers in the West.

Making etchings

The technique of making printed etchings was developed in the 16th century. It involves covering a metal plate with a waxy layer and then drawing onto the plate with an etching needle. The plate is dipped in a bath of acid, which eats into the metal that has had waxed scratched off. Then the rest of the wax is cleaned off, the plate is covered with ink and makes a print. Depending on how long the plate is left in the acid, the lines can be light or dark.

Artists can use etching to create dramatic contrasts between areas of light and dark. Many outstanding artists have used this technique, but perhaps the greatest master of etching was the Dutchman Rembrandt van Rijn. Rembrandt worked in the 17th century. He made over 300 etchings, covering many subjects, including portraits, landscapes, and scenes from daily life.

Rembrandt van Rijn, *Christ Driving the Money Lenders from the Temple* (1635). Rembrandt was a master of the very difficult technique of etching. Notice the range of textures that he has created by using different types of line.

Lithography

Etching is suited to small, detailed studies, but in 1798 a simpler printing technique was discovered. This new technique was called lithography. This process involves drawing with a greasy crayon on a stone or sheet of metal, which is then covered in ink and used as a printing block. Only the areas that are not covered in wax leave a print on the paper. This method can be used several times with different colours to build up a total design.

Lithography works well for simple, bold images. After lithography was discovered, artists used the new technique to make dramatic prints, and to design striking book covers and book illustrations. However, its most exciting use was for printing posters.

Posters for the people

Around the end of the 19th century, two talented artists began to design posters. The Czech artist Alphonse Mucha created a series of posters for Paris theatres. Mucha's posters were usually tall and narrow, and featured female figures, surrounded by patterned borders. Meanwhile, Henri de Toulouse-Lautrec was creating posters for the Moulin Rouge café in Paris. In his striking posters of dancing girls, Toulouse-Lautrec creates swirling shapes and bold blocks of colour.

The posters of Mucha and Toulouse-Lautrec are very different from earlier works of art. They were meant to have a powerful impact when they were viewed from a distance. They were also aimed to appeal to a very wide range of people. Thanks to the new technology of lithography, art could be brought to a much wider audience.

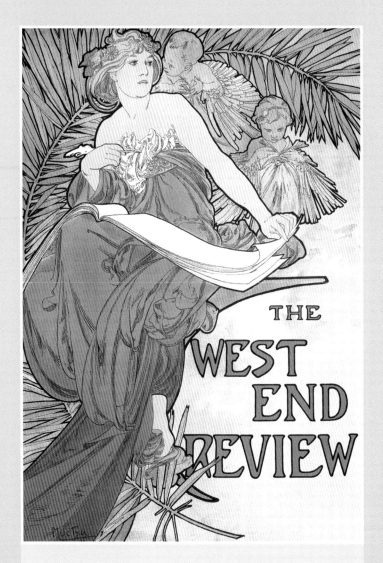

Alphonse Mucha made this poster in 1898, using colour lithography. This new technique allowed artists to create much larger printed works than before.

Screen-printing

The technique of screen-printing was developed in the early 20th century. Screen-printers use a wooden frame with a sheet of silk or polyester fabric stretched over it to form a screen. On this screen, the artist uses a kind of glue to paint a design that covers the parts of the screen where the ink is not meant to go. Then ink is squeezed through the screen onto a sheet of paper, using a "squeegee". This process is repeated several times, with different screens, using different coloured inks.

Screen-printing can be done very quickly and easily. Prints produced by this method are usually bold and dramatic – ideal for large-scale, exciting images. Ever since the 1950s, artists have used screen-printing techniques to create posters and large-scale works of art, and also to print images on T-shirts.

Andy Warhol

One of the best-known users of the screen-print method is the American artist Andy Warhol. In the 1960s, he produced a famous series of images of Marilyn Monroe. Working from a photograph of the Hollywood star, he created prints that all show the same picture of Marilyn but are all printed in different colour combinations.

In his portraits of Marilyn, Warhol deliberately turns his back on the methods of the traditional portrait painters. Instead of creating a single work that an artist has worked on for many months, Warhol creates "instant" images that do not directly involve the artist's hand. This leads the viewer to ask several questions: "What is the role of the artist?"; "What makes good art?", and even "What is art?" Warhol's mass-produced screen prints could also be a comment on the shallow and short-lived nature of the world of celebrities.

Roy Lichtenstein

Around the same time as Andy Warhol was making his screen prints, another American artist was experimenting with different printing effects. Roy Lichtenstein adapted a type of printing known as the "Benday dot system", which was used in cheap comic books. The system used a mechanical printer to print dots of red, yellow, and blue, which were mixed together to make a range of tones.

Lichtenstein painted in a comic-book style, using Benday dots, which he enlarged and exaggerated. Like Andy Warhol, he was asking many questions through his work: "Should comic-book art be considered as real art?"; "Does it matter that the artist does not have a style of his own?", and again "What is art?"

Andy Warhol, *Marilyn Monroe* (1967). Warhol said "... with silk screening you pick a photograph, blow it up, transfer it in glue onto silk, and then roll ink across it so the ink goes through the silk but not through the glue. That way you get the same image, slightly different each time. It was all so simple, quick, and chancy. I was thrilled with it."

Measuring time

For thousands of years, people have constructed clocks to measure the time. The Ancient Egyptians, Greeks, and Romans all made simple **sundials**. This tradition continued in medieval Europe, where sculptors often carved a sundial from stone as a centrepiece for a garden.

Public and private clocks

In the 14th century, the first mechanical clock was built in England. Soon, most cities in Europe had a large clock. Paintings of cities in the late Middle Ages often feature a tall clock tower.

A simple carved stone sundial made by the Romans in modern-day Tunisia. The lines carved on the dial each represent an hour. Originally this sundial would have had a metal rod set in the centre of the carved semi-circle. When the sun shone, the rod would have cast a shadow over the dial, showing the time of day.

In the 15th century, some rich people began to have clocks in their homes. Wealthy people competed with each other to own more and more elaborate clocks. In the 18th and 19th centuries, clock-makers in France made some extraordinary clocks that were also works of sculpture. French "ormolu" clocks were made from gold and marble, and often included sculpted figures.

The art of clock-making still continues today, as designers create some very imaginative shapes and clock faces.

Clocks in art

Many artists have included clocks in their paintings as a symbol of passing time and the shortness of human life.

The 20th century Spanish artist Salvador Dalî was especially fascinated with the idea of clocks and time.

In his dreamlike images, he shows floppy clock faces, stretched out and bent, and sometimes even hanging from the branches of trees. There are many ways to interpret Dali's distorted images of clocks. Perhaps he is trying in his art to break free from the strict rules of time? Or perhaps he is indicating that time works differently in his fantasy world?

An Arab water clock

By the 12th century, some Arab metal-workers were fashioning elaborate water clocks. One Turkish painting from this period shows a remarkable mechanical clock with many moving parts, all driven by water. Every half hour, a bird whistled, a ball dropped into a dragon's mouth, and man riding on an elephant beat on a drum. The artist made a detailed drawing of the clock and described how it worked. He was clearly fascinated by this extraordinary piece of machinery.

Salvador Dali, *The Persistence of Memory* (1931). This surreal image suggests a land in which time no longer has any meaning. The three clock faces are floppy, almost dead objects, and the watch case contains loose screws.

Studying the skies, exploring the Earth

Thousands of years ago, people discovered that the stars were in different positions in the sky at different times of year. Some early people used their knowledge of the movement of the stars and planets to create calendars. Others studied the positions of the stars in the sky to help them sail their boats and ships. Gradually, people developed special instruments for studying the stars and for **navigating** the oceans. They also created maps of the heavens and the land.

Mayan astronomers

The Maya people lived in Central America from around 1500 BCE to 200 CE. They built observatories where **astronomer**-priests could study the skies. Using their knowledge of the stars, the priests decided which days important festivals should be held on. Mayan sculptors made elaborate calendars from stone, carved with symbols and images of the gods, and painted in bright colours. The calendars were a way of understanding and organizing time. They were also beautifully made works of art.

Arab scientists and explorers

During the Middle Ages, Arab scholars established a tradition of studying the skies. Meanwhile, explorers sailed from the Middle East to distant lands, such as China, Africa, and India, using special instruments to help them find their way. The knowledge they gained was used by Arab geographers to create detailed maps of the world.

This painting from an **Islamic** manuscript shows astronomers and geographers using instruments, such as a globe, clock, astrolabe, and compasses and dividers.

Arab astrolabes

Arab craft workers created a range of metal instruments for astronomers and navigators to use. These early navigation instruments include silver and brass astrolabes. An astrolabe is an instrument for measuring the height of stars and planets, which was also used to help sailors navigate at night. The astrolabes were very finely made and covered with detailed engravings. As well as being useful tools, they were fine examples of skilled craft work.

Some Arab astronomers recorded their discoveries in manuscripts. These hand-written books were often illustrated with detailed diagrams of stars and **constellations**. Some manuscripts also showed pictures of the astronomers at work.

One manuscript painting shows a group of astronomers and geographers working in a library in Istanbul, in present-day Turkey. All the scientists use different instruments. The instruments include a globe, a **set square**, and a **pair of compasses**. Another painting shows astronomers working on a large-scale wooden model. Some are using measuring rods to help them make their calculations, and all of them are working as a team, each with their own task to perform. In these busy pictures of scientists at work, there is a sense of excitement about the act of discovery.

An Islamic astrolabe dating from the 14th century. The dials on an astrolabe could be adjusted to calculate the height of stars and planets.

Explorers from Europe

By the 15th century, many people in Europe had become interested in exploring the world. They copied the skills of the Arab astronomers and navigators, and made scientific instruments, such as astrolabes (see page 27) and **compasses**.

Explorers like Christopher Columbus used instruments and maps to help them reach unexplored lands. They recorded what they saw, and geographers created maps.

Many of these early maps featured images of explorers' ships. Some maps also included pictures of strange sea monsters.

Holbein's ambassadors

In 1533, the German artist Hans Holbein painted a double portrait of two rich, well-educated Frenchmen. This painting later became known as *The Ambassadors*. It provides some valuable clues about the science and technology of the Tudor age.

Hans Holbein, *The Ambassadors* (1533). This painting is filled with scientific instruments. It also contains a fascinating optical trick. If you close your right eye and look carefully at the bottom of the picture, you will see that the artist has painted a human skull.

Recording Antarctica

From 1914 to 1916, a young photographer produced a dramatic visual record of a voyage of exploration. Ernest Shackleton hired Frank Hurley to record his expedition to Antarctica. Hurley produced a series of black-and-white photographs and wrote notes to accompany his pictures. His notes sometimes describe the activities of the team, and also discuss the weather and the appearance of the ice. The photos give a very real sense of what it was like to be part of the Antarctic expedition.

In the painting, the two young men lean against a desk that is covered with books and instruments. On the upper shelf of the desk is a celestial (heavenly) globe, which shows the stars and planets. There is also a portable sundial and other instruments used for studying the stars and measuring time. Among the objects on the lower shelf is a book of arithmetic and a globe showing the Earth. These objects reveal that the 16th century was a time of exciting possibilities for wealthy young men. It was a time when they could travel widely and study astronomy, science, and geography.

Images of explorers

Voyages of exploration have inspired artists for centuries. Painters have produced many portraits of explorers with their maps and globes. One of the most famous of these portraits shows Captain James Cook, who reached Australia in 1770. Captain Cook is shown in his uniform, studying a map of the South Pacific Ocean. The map has almost no land marked on it and behind the captain's shoulder there is a view of a wide and empty ocean. The portrait gives a sense of Captain Cook's spirit of adventure, as he explored the unknown waters of the South Seas.

A 17th-century map of Europe. Early maps showed the extent of people's knowledge about the world. They were often also stunning works of art.

Medicine and the human body

From the time of the earliest civilizations, people have tried to understand the mysteries of the human body. They have also tried to find ways to cure diseases. Meanwhile, artists through the ages have shown doctors at work. Some artists have also taken a great interest in the human body. They have tried to learn what happens inside the body so that they can show bodies more accurately in their art.

Chinese acupuncture

Some Ancient Chinese scholars studied the human body very carefully. They worked out a system for treating problems by sticking fine needles into special points on the body. This treatment is known as **acupuncture**. It was first used in China over 4,000 years ago.

Chinese artists created models and paintings of the human body, showing the pressure points for acupuncture. Some of these images are attractive works of art. One painting from around the 16th century shows a man gracefully extending his arm. The man's arm has pressure points marked on it, and lines are drawn on his body to show how these points are linked to his stomach and heart. Another painting from this time shows a doctor practising acupuncture. In this image, both the doctor and his patient seem relaxed and comfortable, as they work together.

Greek and Roman healing

By the time of the Ancient Greeks and Romans, doctors were performing quite difficult operations. They used simple surgical instruments to cut off limbs, sew up wounds, and remove lumps and growths. Meanwhile, scholars invented theories about the way the human body worked. The leading figure in Greek and Roman medicine was Galen, who lived in the 2nd century CE. Galen's ideas of how the body worked were followed for many centuries. Unfortunately, they were not entirely correct.

Some Greek and Roman artists showed doctors at work. A Greek vase from the 5th century BCE shows a doctor's surgery. Patients line up to consult the doctor, who sits on an elegant chair. The doctor holds a small knife and is about to make a cut in a patient's arm. Hanging above the doctor's head is a small cup, which was used to drain blood from the patient. The practice of "cupping" – draining off cups of blood – was often used in Greek and Roman times. Doctors believed that cupping could remove the "poison" of a disease and help people to recover. In fact, it left the patients much weaker than before.

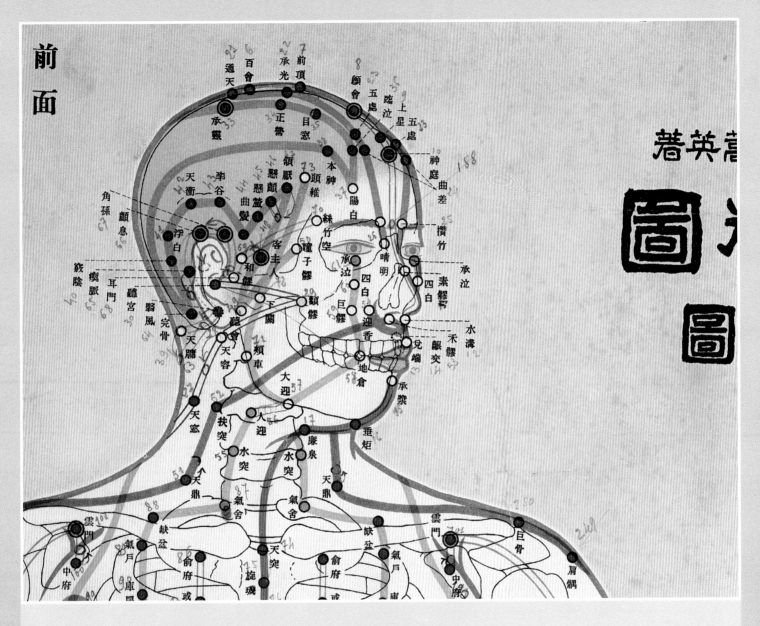

A detail from a Chinese chart, showing the acupuncture points on the human body. This image is based on a chart in an 11th-century guide to acupuncture.

Medieval medicine

After the fall of the Roman Empire in the 5th century CE, there were very few advances in medical knowledge in Europe for the next thousand years. Most people hoped for miracles, and prayed to saints or went on **pilgrimages**. However, doctors continued to treat patients. They also performed operations, although these often had bad results.

Like the Roman artists, medieval artists show doctors cupping their patients to drain away "bad blood". One painting shows a seated man, holding a bowl to catch his blood, while a doctor operates on his eye. Another image shows a painful-looking treatment for a dislocated shoulder. Two assistants hold a pole under the patient's shoulder, while a doctor pulls down hard on his arm.

A new understanding

In the 15th century, some scientists and doctors in Europe began to dissect dead bodies to help them understand how the body worked. This was dangerous work, because dissection was forbidden by the Church (the most important organization in the Middle Ages). However, some determined scientists continued their work and developed the science of anatomy.

An illustration from a medieval herbal, showing a doctor performing an eye operation. The patient is fully conscious and has to be held still by the doctor!

Arab instruments

During the Middle Ages, doctors in the Arab world learned about diseases and became very skilled at operating. A few outstanding doctors recorded their knowledge in hand-written manuscripts. Some of these manuscripts are illustrated with paintings. The paintings show a range of surgical instruments, including saws, knives, and **forceps**.

Michelangelo and Leonardo

Scientists were not the only people who were interested in human anatomy. In the 15th century, some artists studied dead bodies in order to create more realistic works of art. The painter and **sculptor** Michelangelo paid secret visits to a morgue to sketch dead bodies. Another great artist, Leonardo da Vinci, dissected over 30 bodies and made detailed anatomical studies in his sketchbooks.

One page of Leonardo's sketchbook is packed with careful drawings of arms, legs, hands, and feet. Some images show the skeleton, while others reveal the muscles and **ligaments**. All the drawings are incredibly detailed. They are also accompanied by lengthy notes. These remarkable drawings reveal Leonardo's passionate interest in the science of anatomy.

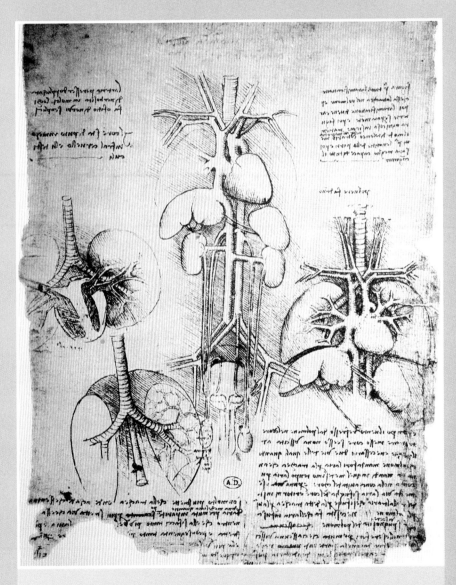

A page from one of Leonardo da Vinci's notebooks, with sketches of human hearts, lungs, and kidneys.

Vesalius and art

In 1543, the **Flemish** scientist Vesalius produced a very important study of human anatomy. It was called *On the Fabric of the Human Body*. Vesalius realized that he needed a trained artist to illustrate his work, so he employed Jan Stephan van Calcar, a student of the famous artist Titian. Van Calcar produced over 200 detailed illustrations for Vesalius. His images are beautiful works of art. They include full-length figures, revealing muscles and organs, but also detailed studies of portions of the human body.

On the title page of *On the Fabric of the Human Body* is a picture by van Calcar and other members of Titian's workshop. It shows Vesalius dissecting a body in an enormous hall, surrounded by hundreds of students. This picture shows the growing interest in the study of anatomy by the mid-16th century.

Surgeons at work

As knowledge of human anatomy increased, surgeons attempted more and more ambitious operations. One very important discovery took place in 1846, when surgeons discovered that a chemical called "ether" could be used as an **anaesthetic** to put patients to sleep for a short time. With their patient completely unconscious, surgeons could perform much more difficult operations.

The US artist Robert C. Hinckley painted the first operation performed under ether. His painting shows an unconscious patient seated in a chair, while the surgeon uses a pair of forceps to remove a lump from the man's neck. The anaesthetist stands at the patient's side holding a flask of ether, ready to give him another dose if it is required. The painting shows the operation being carried out in a lecture room, with an audience of students looking on.

Modern medicine and art

Today's doctors and scientists use a wide range of methods to help them understand what is happening inside people's bodies. X-rays show whether bones are broken, and **MRI scans** reveal if there is damage inside the brain. It is also possible to examine the cells that make up the human body, using a very powerful microscope.

Many of today's artists are inspired by medical science. The American **textile** artist Michael James has produced a series of works based on MRI scans of his own brain. In *Scan*, *Mind's Eye*, and *A Strange Riddle*, James explores the nature of human memory by combining MRI images of the brain with family photographs. The British sculptor Marilene Oliver uses an MRI body scan in her work *Ophelia*. This intriguing work shows the structure of the young woman's body glowing strangely through her clothes. It gives a sense of the mystery of human life.

Thomas Eakins, *The Gross Clinic* (1875). Eakins shows surgeons at work in the gross clinic, the part of a hospital where major operations were carried out. Eakins wanted to show the operation as realistically as possible. However, art critics called the painting "unsightly".

Machines, ships, and trains

In the 1760s, inventors in Britain began to make new machines. These machines changed the way that people worked because they allowed them to do traditional work, such as weaving, very fast. Wealthy businessmen built large factories to house these machines, and people began to work in factories instead of at home.

At first, the new machines were worked by water power, but by the 1700s, steam engines were used to run the machines in the factories. By the 1840s, steam engines were also used to power trains and ships. In order to build the steam engines, trains, and ships, huge amounts of iron were needed. Vast **furnaces** were built to produce the iron. These furnaces were built in towns and cities, close to the factories.

The Industrial Revolution

By the 1850s, the new technology had changed people's lives dramatically. Many people lived in towns, and worked in factories and furnaces. A network of railways had been built in Europe and the United States. People and goods were carried in trains around the country, while steamships carried goods to other parts of the world. All these changes came to be known as the **Industrial Revolution**.

Helpful machinery

In the 1770s, at the beginning of the Industrial Revolution, many people were hopeful about the new inventions. The British painter Joseph Wright reflected this optimistic mood when he painted *An Iron Forge* in 1772. Wright's painting shows a blacksmith using a water powered hammer to shape a piece of metal. Meanwhile, his family gather around to gaze in wonder at the new invention. The painter seems to be saying that, thanks to the new technology, the blacksmith can now do more work, and his family can be well-fed and healthy.

A vision of hell

By the start of the 19th century, many factories and furnaces had been built. In order to earn enough money to survive, workers had to work for very long hours in these noisy and dangerous places. Artists began to paint pictures that reflected the nightmare of the workers' experience.

In 1801, P. J. de Loutherbourg painted *Coalbrookdale by Night*. He showed the fires from the iron furnaces glowing red and orange, and belching out clouds of smoke. In this dramatic painting, de Loutherbourg makes a British industrial town look like a vision of hell.

Joseph Wright, *An Iron Forge* (1772). In Wright's attractive painting the new technology of the water-powered hammer is shown in a very positive light. At this time, the blacksmith's forge had not yet been replaced by the iron **foundry**.

Turner's response

The English artist J. M. W. Turner lived from 1775 to 1851. He loved the British countryside and painted hundreds of pictures of the landscape, but he was also excited by the new methods of transport that were developed during his lifetime.

Images of steam and speed

In the last ten years of his life Turner produced some famous images of trains and steamships. Many people think that these paintings are some of his finest works.

Rain, Steam and Speed was painted in 1844. It shows a steam train crossing a bridge in misty, rainy weather. The tall, dark chimney of the steam engine stands out strongly against the golden, hazy light. Turner gives his painting an exciting sense of energy and movement, which is concentrated in the shape of the steam engine driving forward.

Another dramatic Turner painting is Snowstorm: Steamboat off a Harbour's Mouth, which was painted in 1842. It shows a tiny steamship caught between a wild, whirling wave and a raging sky.

J. M. W. Turner, Rain, Steam and Speed (1844). Turner's painting, featuring a steam train, shows a new industrial landscape. In the background, an old-fashioned river bridge for horse-drawn carriages is a reminder of an age that is disappearing.

The steamship is battered by the storm, but the viewer gets the sense that it will survive. Turner manages to make the ship seem brave and indestructible, as it drives onwards though the waves.

A farewell to sail

In 1838, Turner produced a painting of a beautiful sailing ship being towed by a small steamship; *The Fighting "Temeraire" tugged to her Last Berth to be broken up*. It was one of Turner's favourite works.

In this famous painting, the steam powered tugboat, with its stark, black chimney belching brown smoke is in stark contrast to the pale and ghostly sailing ship. The painting seems to express Turner's mixed feelings about technological progress. It is sad to see the end of the beautiful old sailing ships, but the sturdy steamship is performing a necessary job. The scene takes place at sunset – perhaps to suggest that the sun is setting on the great age of sailing.

J. M. W. Turner, *Snowstorm: Steamboat off a Harbour's Mouth* (1842). A steamship battles its way through a storm, staining the sky brown with its smoke. Turner's new and energetic style of painting seems to match his powerful new subject.

Powerful impressions

In his later paintings, Turner's style of painting became much less precise. Instead of showing the exact details of what he saw, Turner concentrated on the impression that a scene made on his senses. In some ways, Turner's approach to painting is similar to the approach of the **Impressionist** artists, such as Claude Monet (see page 40), who were painting 20 years later.

Monet's trains

Just like Turner, Claude Monet was a landscape painter who was fascinated by trains. Monet lived in France from 1840 to 1926, at a time when railway travel had become an accepted part of daily life. Monet painted many scenes of busy railway stations. He also showed trains travelling through fields and steaming over bridges.

Monet was a leading member of the Impressionist Movement, and his images of trains concentrate on the impressions that they made on his senses. For Monet, steam trains were beautiful things. His engines are not detailed, but are instantly recognizable.

They have elegant, tall black chimneys, and seem to blend into the countryside as they send out billows of pure white smoke. All Monet's railway paintings give a sense of the artist's delight in the engine's energy.

The machine age

By the early 20th century, machines had become an essential part of modern living. Factories were filled with gleaming metal machinery, people travelled by train and bicycle, and the first cars were being built. Many artists of this period were fascinated by machinery. Some created very positive images, but others showed the negative effects that machines had on people's lives.

Claude Monet, *Saint-Lazare Station* (1877). Monet painted many views of this busy station in Paris. In his paintings of steam engines, he aimed to show the excitement and adventure of railway journeys.

Picabia and Léger

Two French artists who concentrated on machinery in their work were Francis Picabia and Fernand Léger. Picabia produced almost **abstract** paintings of **pistons**, **cranks**, **cogs**, and **levers**. Some of his machine paintings are witty comments on the relationship between men and women, and the way they react to each other.

Like Picabia, Léger made many studies of machinery. He also painted portraits of people with machines. Several of his paintings feature people with bicycles, while *Red Time Travellers* shows a group of people on a time machine. One of Léger's most famous paintings is *The Builders* (1950). It shows men at work high up in the clouds surrounded by steel girders, ladders, and chains. Everything in their world is machine-made and even the builders seem like robots, working smoothly with the machinery. However, Léger's vision of the machine age seems generally to be a positive one, where people and machinery work in harmony.

Fernand Léger, *The Builders* (1950). This painting may symbolize the rebuilding of France after World War II, which ended in 1945.

Duchamp's "readymades"

In the early years of the 20th century, the French artist and sculptor Marcel Duchamp created a series of sculptures made from pieces of machinery and domestic equipment. These objects include a coat stand, a urinal, and a bicycle wheel mounted on a wooden stool. Duchamp called these works "readymades" because they had already been made in a factory. By presenting these pieces as works of art, Duchamp was questioning whether something made in a factory could be seen as art. He was also asking the question, "What is art?"

Progress in America

American industry really took off in the 20th century. Massive foundries supplied vast amounts of steel to build railways and skyscrapers, and, in 1913, Henry Ford set up the first production line for cars. One of the leading artists to record this rapid growth in technology was the painter and photographer, Charles Sheeler.

Sheeler invented the term "precisionism" to explain his art. He showed industrial buildings and machines as precisely as he could, with no expressive strokes of paint. In 1927, the Ford Motor Company hired Sheeler to spend six weeks taking photographs in its factory at River Rouge, near Detroit. Sheeler's famous work *River Rouge Plant Stamping Press* shows a vast machine towering over its tiny human operator. Sheeler claimed that his images showed the glory of the new machine age, but this picture also has a frightening side. The factory worker seems like a slave serving a huge, mechanical master.

Charles Sheeler, *River Rouge Plant* (1932). Sheeler's painting of the Ford Motor factory shows modern buildings like machines, perfectly designed to perform their tasks. The painting does not include any people – instead it shows a train delivering goods to the factory.

Industrial materials

Several sculptors have used industrial materials and machinery in their work. In the 1940s, the Swiss artist Jean Tinguely started to use pieces of machinery to create sculptures. He attached small electric motors to his sculptures so that they became working machines. Some of Tinguely's machines moved along the ground, some spun around, and some played music. One very famous work, called *Homage to New York* (1959), was specially designed to destroy itself when it was set in motion. Tinguely's playful sculptures take a light-hearted look at the usually serious world of machinery and construction.

The American sculptor David Smith trained as a metal worker in a car factory in 1925. Later, he used these skills in his art. Smith created sculptures from **welded** steel, and his works often included scrap metal items and industrial parts that he ordered from manufacturers' catalogues. Many of Smith's works have a positive message, and express the progress of the industrial age. However, Smith also shows the cruel and destructive nature of machinery, through his use of harsh shapes, such as jagged saws.

In recent years, two famous sculptors have worked with industrial materials. The American Richard Serra creates massive works from rusted steel.

He draws on his experience of working in steel mills and shipyards when he was young. The British sculptor Anthony Caro constructs giant metal structures connected with massive bolts. His works include industrial parts and often resemble giant pieces of machinery.

In the late 1970s, Anthony Caro produced a series of *Emma* sculptures, named after the Emma Lakes in Saskatchewan, Canada, where Caro held a two week artists' workshop. All the sculptures were made from scrap metal materials.

Cars, planes, and rockets

Ever since the first automobiles were manufactured in the 1890s, artists and photographers have been inspired to produce images of cars. Some artists have tried to give an impression of the car's speed, while others have shown the experience of being inside a moving car. A few artists have decorated cars themselves, creating vehicles that are also works of art.

Movement and speed

From 1912 to 1914, the Italian artist Giacomo Balla produced a series of works showing motorbikes and cars in rapid motion. One of these paintings is called *Abstract speed – a car has passed*.

It shows a passing car as a series of black shapes moving across the painting. Blue segments spin out of the car, representing waves of energy.

Balla belonged to a group of artists known as the **Futurists**. Their aim was to look forward to the future and celebrate the noise, movement, and excitement of machines. The Futurists were especially excited by the motor car. In 1909, a leading member of the Futurist movement, Filippo Marinetti, published a statement praising the "roaring automobile" and saying, "The world's splendour has been enriched by a new beauty: the beauty of speed."

Giacomo Balla, *The Speed of an Automobile* (1913). Running across the picture are a series of repeated circles, representing the car's wheels, while a series of geometric shapes give a powerful sense of energy and speed.

Roy Lichtenstein, *In the Car* (1963). In this "portrait on the move", Roy Lichtenstein deliberately uses a comic book style, to suggest fast-moving action.

Inside the car

In 1963, Roy Lichtenstein created *In the Car*. It shows a close-up of a driver and passenger, seen through the passenger's window. The window has speed lines marked on it, so the viewer gets the sense that they can only see inside the car for a moment. In this famous picture, Lichtenstein is exploring the idea that people in their cars exist in a separate, **isolated** world. *In the Car* has been seen as a comment on the isolation of modern life.

Decorating cars

In 1975, the American artist Alexander Calder painted a design on his friend's car. The friend later raced the car at Le Mans, in France. This tradition has continued and has allowed many people to experience "art on the move". Artists who have created similar moving works of art include Andy Warhol, Frank Stella, Roy Lichtenstein, Robert Rauschenberg, and David Hockney. The British painter David Hockney turned his design into a comment on the experience of driving a car. The side view reveals the body of the driver at the wheel and a little dog is shown in the back seat.

Trying to fly

Many artists and writers have been fascinated by the idea of flying. In the 16th century, the great Italian artist and inventor, Leonardo da Vinci, produced a series of sketches illustrating his ideas for a flying machine. Unfortunately, none of Leonardo's ideas worked, and it took another 200 years before people managed to build a machine to get them off the ground.

Early flights

In the 1780s, people began to take to the air in hot air balloons. Artists recorded these early flights in coloured prints, which became very popular. Some of these prints show some remarkable flying machines. In one print, a balloon crosses the English Channel equipped with a tail fin and "air oars"!

In 1903, the Wright brothers in America became the first people to fly an aeroplane for a controlled, sustained period of time. Six years later, Louis Bleriot flew his bi-plane over the English Channel. The painter Robert Delaunay was among the crowds welcoming the triumphant aviator back to France. Delaunay spent many hours sketching the early planes. According to his wife, "he watched the take-offs with joyous eyes".

Robert Delaunay, *Homage to Bleriot* (1914). In this colourful painting, the sky appears to be filled with planes. The vivid colours and dramatic shapes express Delaunay's excitement about this new method of transport.

Roy Lichtenstein, *Whaam!* (1963). Lichtestein's comic-book style gives a strong sense of drama and action. It is an ideal way to show the speed, noise, and danger of a jet plane.

In 1914, Delaunay painted *Homage to Bleriot*. This colourful painting includes several images of Bleriot's plane, some close-up and others in the distance. The painting is dominated by circular patterns, suggesting the movement of the plane's propellers.

Jet planes

By the mid-20th century, jet engines had replaced propellers, and planes had become sleek, powerful machines. The overwhelming sense of power, speed, and noise produced by a jet plane is brilliantly expressed by Roy Lichtenstein in his painting *Whaam!* (1963). The painting shows a fighter jet racing through the sky and then exploding in a burst of flames.

Images of space

In the 1950s, the space programme began. America and Russia sent rockets into space, and in 1969, astronauts walked on the Moon. Photographers have captured some historic moments in space travel, showing rockets taking off and astronauts floating through space. The photograph of astronaut Buzz Aldrin walking on the Moon has become one of the most famous images of the 20th century. It reflects an astonishing human achievement.

The communications revolution

At the start of the 19th century, two very important inventions were made. In 1826, Joseph Niécpe took the first photograph. Then, in 1876, Alexander Graham Bell invented the telephone. Around the end of the 19th century, radio and moving photography were discovered, and the first public demonstration of a television took place in 1926.

Meanwhile, computers were also developing. The first computers were made in the 19th century, but they were large machines that worked with cogs and wheels. The first personal computers were sold in the 1970s, and the World Wide Web developed in the 1990s. By the start of the 21st century, people had an amazing range of technology to help them communicate wherever they went.

Artists responded to developments in technology in different ways. Some artists produced works of art showing new inventions. Many others used the new technology to create a different kind of art.

Early telephones

By the 20th century, the telephone was making an appearance in art. The Spanish artist Salvador Dalî was fascinated by telephones, and he pictured them in some very surprising ways.

His sculpture *Lobster Telephone* is a telephone with a lobster resting on top of the hand-piece. The painting *Melting Phone* shows a telephone hand-piece hanging in a tree, slowly melting into the ground. Dalî also painted dry, empty landscapes with a set of telephone poles and wires leading to a giant telephone hand-piece, stuck in a tree.

It is difficult to know exactly why Dalî showed telephones in his art. His paintings explore the **subconscious mind**. For him, perhaps the telephone represents the way he communicates with other people, or the way the world sends messages to him?

Salvador Dalî, *Lobster Telephone* (1936). This surreal image can be interpreted in many ways. Why do you think Dali chose to combine a lobster with the telepone?

Eugène Atget began taking photographs in the 1890s, when the art of photography was still in its experimental stage. His photographs, such as this study of pumpkin plants, were taken with a simple box camera, using only natural light.

Photography and art

From the very early days of photography, people realized that it was not just a scientific invention. Photography could also be a form of art. Soon, photographers were creating beautiful landscapes and portraits. Artist-photographers experimented with different **exposure times** for film. They used a range of different types of cameras and films, and tried out different methods of developing and treating photographs, in order to get special effects.

Artists today are still pushing the boundaries of what they can achieve through photography. Recently, artists have started using digital cameras and computer programs to create a new kind of photographic art. These new tools allow artists to alter colours and shapes, to combine images from many different shots, and to incorporate text in their pictures. These exciting new forms of technology have allowed artists to look at the world in a different way.

49

Cinema and art

In 1895, the Lumière brothers invented the cinematographic camera in France. This invention led to the birth of cinema. Cinema offered great opportunities for film directors, scriptwriters, set designers, and actors.

One famous early film was *Modern Times*, which appeared in 1936 and starred Charlie Chaplin. *Modern Times* is an attack on the machine age. It includes a famous scene in which Charlie frantically tries to keep up with a factory production line.

A still from Charlie Chaplin's movie *Modern Times* (1936). Chaplin's famous film shows the human workers in a factory as tiny, unimportant cogs in a vast machine.

Today's film directors are constantly experimenting with new technology and using computers to create special effects. In 1995, *Toy Story* made history as the first film to be made entirely on computer. More recently, films like *Shrek* and *The Incredibles* have developed the art of **computer animation** to the point where the characters and scenes can seem completely solid and life-like.

Video, light, and sound

In the 1980s, portable video cameras were invented, and more and more artists began to make their own films. Projectors showing the films were set up in special rooms inside art galleries, and artists' films became known as "video **installations**".

Bill Viola is one of the world's leading video artists. Even though he uses the latest technology, Viola's works have a sense of timelessness. They focus on universal human experiences, such as birth and death, and are often inspired by great paintings of the past. *Going Forth By Day* (2002) is a five-part video work examining cycles of birth, death, and rebirth. It is based on a series of wall-paintings by the 14th-century artist Giotto.

Other artists use video technology in different ways. Dan Flavin creates "light sculptures" from tubes of fluorescent light. Bruce Nauman often uses sound recordings, creating "bands of sound" for his audience to travel through.

What next?

In recent years, artists have drawn on images produced by scientific research. Diagrams of atoms, photographs of cells, and scans of body parts have all been used as the starting points for works of art.

Meanwhile, other artists have produced works of art using the latest computer technology. Some artists create "software art" – producing and printing works of art with the help of a computer. Other artists have worked on "Internet art". These Internet projects can involve searching the Internet for information, and forming a kind of "information tree".

It is impossible to predict what directions art will take in the future. But one thing is certain – whatever new discoveries are made, artists will respond to them. They will use their art to comment on progress in science and technology. They will also use the latest technology to create exciting works of art.

Map and Further reading

GERMANY
HOLLAND
UNITED
KINGDOM
BELGIUM
FRANCE
EUROPE
ITALY
SPAIN
GREECE
EGYPT
SAUDI
ARABIA
IRAN
RUSSIA
ASIA
CHINA
INDIA
UNITED STATES
OF AMERICA
MEXICO
Atlantic Ocean
Pacific Ocean
Pacific Ocean
SOUTH
AMERICA
AFRICA
Indian Ocean
AUSTRALASIA

Map of the world

This map shows you roughly where in the world some key works of art referred to in this book were produced. The countries marked on the map relate to entries in the timeline, opposite.

Further reading

History in Art series
(Raintree, 2005)

Directions in Art series
(Heinemann Library, 2003)

Art in History series
(Heinemann Library, 2001)

Eyewitness Art: Looking at Paintings, Jude Welton, (Dorling Kindersley, 1994)

Timeline

This timeline provides approximate dates for some key works of art, to give a rough idea of when the works were produced. The entries are linked to countries marked on the map of the world, opposite.

BCE

c.20,000 Cave painters show hunters with spears, bows, and arrows (France)

c.11,000 People in the Middle East make and decorate pots

c.3500 Sumerian artists show chariots with wheels (modern-day Iran)

c.2800 The Ancient Egyptians build pyramids and write hieroglyphs

c.500 Greeks start to build temples

Greek artists show doctors at work

c.100 The Ancient Romans use concrete to construct massive buildings

Mayan sculptors carve calendars (modern-day Mexico)

CE

c.600 Artists in China start to make woodblock prints

c.1000 People in Europe start to build castles and cathedrals. Artists show medieval builders at work.

Arab craft workers make astrolabes and other navigation instruments

c.1300 People in Europe start making clocks

The art of manuscript illumination flourishes in Europe

1450s Artists in Europe start making woodcuts for printed books

c.1500 Leonardo da Vinci makes detailed studies of human anatomy (Italy)

1543 Vesalius produces *On the Fabric of the Human Body* (modern-day Belgium)

1632 Rembrandt van Rijn paints *The Anatomy Lesson of Dr Tulp* (Holland)

1770s Artists begin to show industrial machines

1844 J. M. W. Turner paints *Rain, Steam and Speed* (UK)

1850s Hiroshige makes over 100 prints of Edo in Tokyo (Japan)

1913 Giacoma Balla paints *The Speed of an Automobile* (Italy)

Marcel Duchamp makes his first "readymade" (France)

1914 Robert Delaunay paints *Homage to Bleriot* (France)

1919 Joseph Stella makes his first painting of Brooklyn Bridge (USA)

1920s Charles Sheeler photographs the Ford Motor factory (USA)

1936 *Modern Times* is released (USA)

1936 Salvador Dalî creates *Lobster Telephone* (Spain)

1950 Fernand Léger paints *The Builders* (France)

1960s Andy Warhol makes his prints of Marilyn Monroe (USA)

1963 Roy Lichtenstein produces *In the Car* (USA)

1970s Dan Flavin creates light installations using fluorescent light tubes (USA)

1990s Anthony Caro creates works from rusted machinery parts (UK)

1995 *Toy Story* is the first film to be made entirely on computer (USA)

2002 Bill Viola makes the video work *Going Forth by Day* (USA)

Glossary

abstract showing an idea rather than a thing

acupuncture a way of treating illness by pricking parts of the body with small needles

anaesthetic a drug or gas given to a patient before an operation to prevent them from feeling pain

anatomy the structure of a human or animal body

archaeologist someone who studies the past by uncovering old objects or buildings

architect someone who designs buildings and checks that they are built correctly

architectural to do with the way that buildings are designed

astronomer someone who studies the stars and planets

Buddhist someone who follows the religon of Buddhism. Buddhists believe that you should not become too attached to material things. They also believe that you live many lives in different bodies.

chisel a tool with a flat end, used for shaping stone and wood

cocoon a covering made from silky threads that protects some caterpillars while they are hatching into a butterfly or a moth

cog one of the teeth on the edge of a wheel that turns machinery

colosseum a massive amphitheatre (circular stadium) built by the Romans

communications methods used to share information between people. TV, radio, and telephones are all types of communication.

compass an instrument that helps you work out what direction you are going. A compass has a magnetic needle that always points north.

computer animation pictures created by using a computer

constellation a group of stars that form a shape or pattern

crank a rod in a machine, used for winding or lifting

dissect to cut up a body or another structure in order to learn more about it

engraving a design carved into a hard surface such as wood or metal

exposure time length of time that light is allowed to reach photographic film

Flemish from Flanders (modern-day Belgium)

forceps a kind of pliers, used in medical operations

foundries factories where metal is made

furnace a very large, hot oven, used for making metal

Futurists a group of artists who looked forward to the future and celebrated the excitement of machines. The Futurist Movement began in Italy in the early 20th century.

geometric using forms found in geometry, such as a square, a triangle or a circle

girder an iron rod used in buildings to support floors and roofs

hieroglyphs picture symbols used in some ancient forms of writing

Impressionist a style of painting in which artists try to show the impression that something has on their senses

Industrial Revolution a period of history (beginning in the 18th century) when machines and engines became very important

installation an artwork involving sound, light or video that is installed (set up) in a gallery

Islamic the civilization developed by Muslims, who follow the religion Islam

isolated cut off

lever a bar or handle used to lift something

ligament a band of strong tissue connects bone to bone

mallet a heavy wooden hammer

manuscript a hand-written book

medieval belonging to the period from approximately 1000 CE to 1450 CE

Middle Ages the period of history between approximately 1000 CE and 1450 CE

mortar a kind of cement

mosaic a picture or pattern made up of tiny pieces of coloured stone or glass

MRI scan a picture of the brain produced by a scanning machine. The intials MRI stand for 'magnetic resonance imaging'.

navigation travelling on land and by sea with the help of instruments to guide you

pair of compasses instrument with two legs connected by a flexible joint, used for drawing circles

pigment paint made from natural materials such as earth

pilgrimage a journey to a holy place

piston a rod in a steam engine that is connected to the engine's wheels and helps to make the wheels go round

prehistoric belonging to a time millions of years ago, before history was written down

pulley a simple lifting machine made from wheels and ropes

scribe someone who copied books by hand, before printing was invented

scripture holy writings

scroll a rolled-up piece of paper or parchment with writing on it

sculptor someone who makes works of art from stone, wood, metal or other materials

set square an instrument that makes it possible to draw right angles

silk worm a caterpillar that spins a cocoon of silk threads

subconscious mind the part of the mind that works without people being aware of it

sundial an instrument that shows the time by using shadows cast by the sun

textile fabric or material

welded fixed together with metal, that has been melted and then allowed to harden

winch a cable wound around a wheel, that is used for lifting things

Index

Titles in the *Through Artists' Eyes* series include:

Hardback   1 406 20151 0

Hardback   1 406 20153 7

Hardback   1 406 20152 9

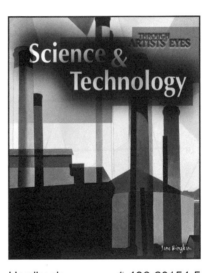

Hardback   1 406 20154 5

Hardback   1 406 20150 2

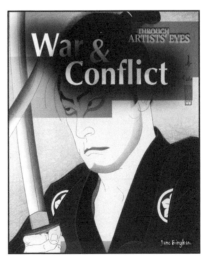

Hardback   1 406 20149 9

Find out about other raintree titles on our website www.raintreelibrary.co.uk